KING ST.

Set Three
BOOK I

Save the Pub

Save the Pub
King Street: Readers Set Three - Book 1
Copyright © Iris Nunn 2014

Text: Iris Nunn
Editor: June Lewis

Published in 2014 by Gatehouse Media Limited

ISBN: 978-1-84231-126-4

British Library Cataloguing-in-Publication Data:
A catalogue record for this book is available from the British Library

Sid was fed up.

Trade at the King's Arms was bad.

He had to think of a way
to bring the customers in.

"I can sell beer,
but there is no life in the bar.
They stand here with long faces
and nobody smiles," he said.

Fred used to play the piano,
Tom used to tell jokes
and Sam used to come in with his dog,
but not now.

They have all gone to the Black Bull
in town.

I miss them all.

The pub will have to close.

Then Sid had a plan.

He spoke to Shane at the bar
as he wiped the bar down.
"Can you play the drums?"

He spoke to Steve as he played darts.
"What music can you play?"

"I can play sax," said Steve.

He spoke to Brenda, his wife.
"You sing well.
Will you sing with Steve and Shane
in the pub?"

They all got together to form a band for Saturday nights.

The pub soon filled with customers.

Faces lit up as the band played.

Sid pulled pints and sold crisps and nuts.

He was rushed off his feet.

"Brenda is singing.
Steve is playing sax.
Shane is on the drums.
I will need a lot more help now."

It was much better with live music
and Brenda was the star!